VOCAL SELECTIONS

"YOU'RE A GOOD MAN, CHARLIE BROWN"

MUSIC AND LYRICS BY CLARK GESNER

T0053078

CONTENTS

A PUBLICATION OF
MPL COMMUNICATIONS, INC.
http://www.mplcommunications.com

EXCLUSIVELY DISTRIBUTED BY

HAL•LEONARD® CORPORATION
7777 W. BLUEMOUND RD. P.O. BOX 13819 MILWAUKEE, WI 53213

YOU'RE A GOOD MAN, CHARLIE BROWN

Words and Music by
CLARK GESNER

You're A Good Man, Charlie Brown - 4

MY BLANKET AND ME

Linus: Where's my blanket?
Come on, 'fess up. When I find the wise guy who took my blanket,
I'm gonna give him such a....
Oh, here it is....

Words and Music by
CLARK GESNER

Soft, gentle, playful

Linus: (Sigh)

Linus: De - light - ful.

La - de - da - de,

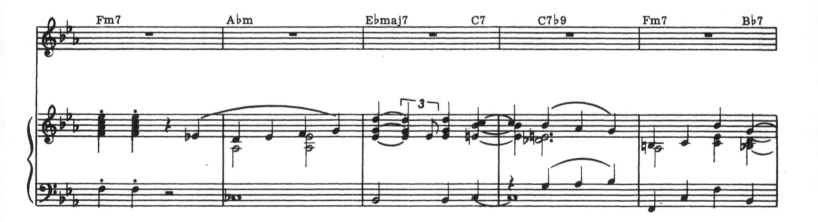

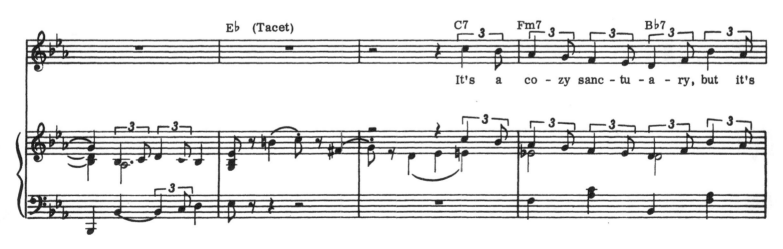

My Blanket And Me - 5

far from nec - ess - ar - y, 'cause I'm just as self - re - li - ant as be -

fore. As a sim - ple dem - on - stra - tion of my

in - de - pen - dent sta - tion I will go and leave my blank - et on the

floor. Yes, I'll walk a - way and leave it, 'Though I

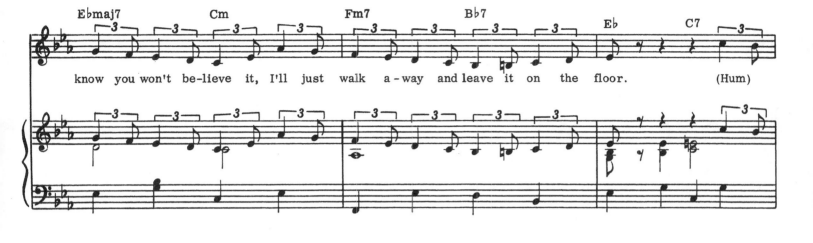

know you won't be-lieve it, I'll just walk a-way and leave it on the floor. (Hum)

(Hum) (Hum grows tenser until it finally
explodes as he

grabs for blanket) Don't ever let me do
that again.

(Whistle)

Got you back a-gain,

THE DOCTOR IS IN

Words and Music by
CLARK GESNER

The Doctor Is In - 5

The Doctor Is In - 5

SCHROEDER

Words and Music by
CLARK GESNER
with Apologies to Beethoven

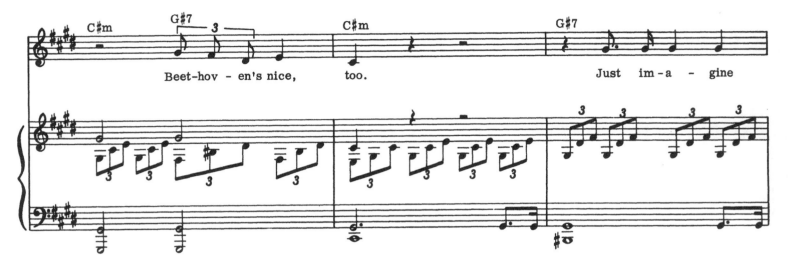

Beet-hov - en's nice, too. Just im - a - gine

what would you think if some-day you and I should get mar - ried?

Would-n't you like that if some-day we two should get mar - ried?

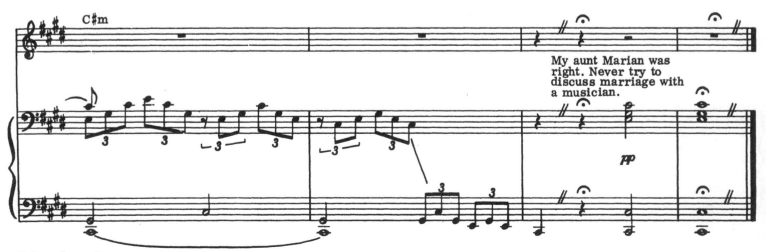

My aunt Marian was right. Never try to discuss marriage with a musician.

Schroeder - 3

SNOOPY

Words and Music by
CLARK GESNER

22

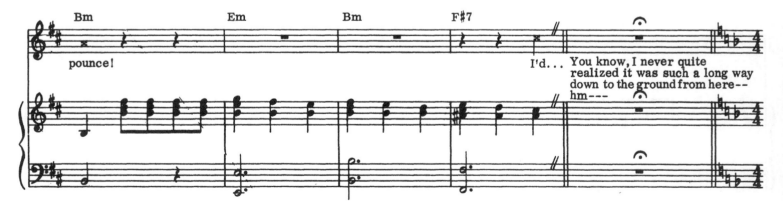

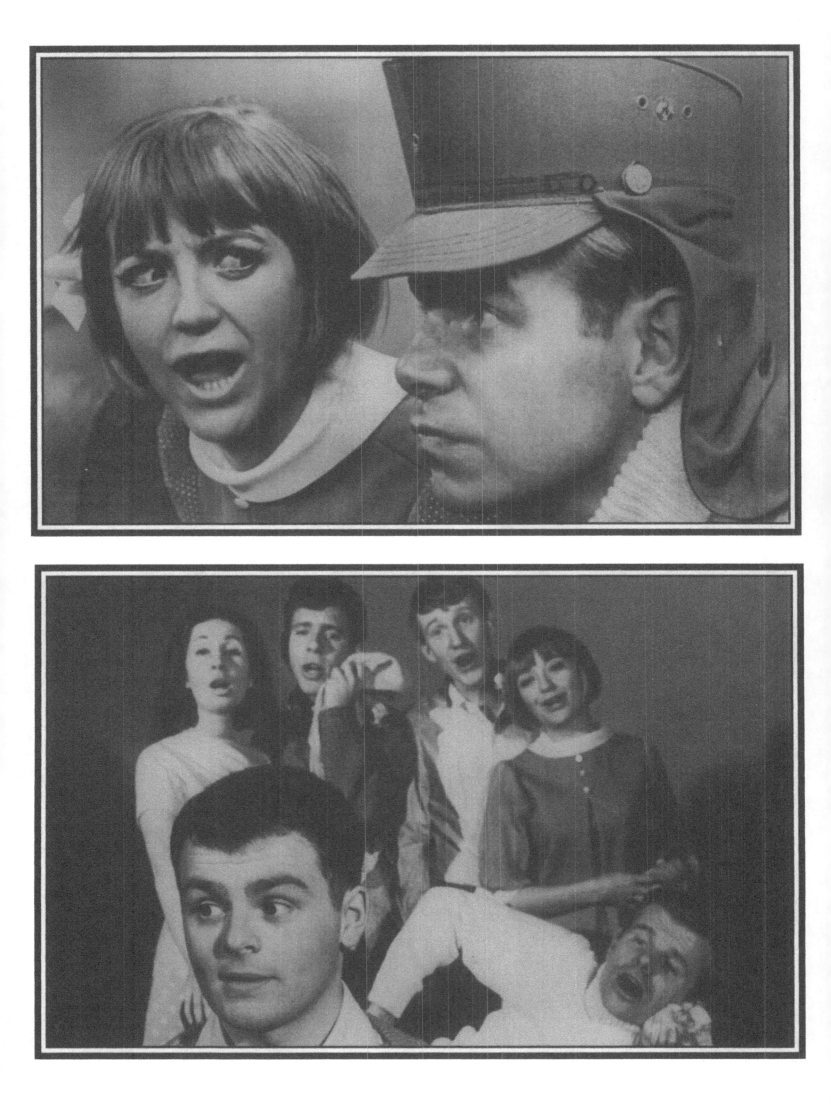

THE BASEBALL GAME

Words and Music by
CLARK GESNER

March tempo

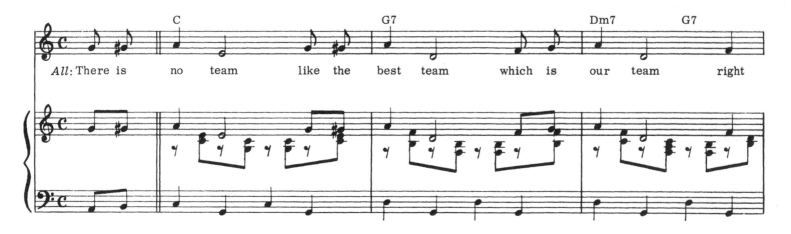

All: There is no team like the best team which is our team right

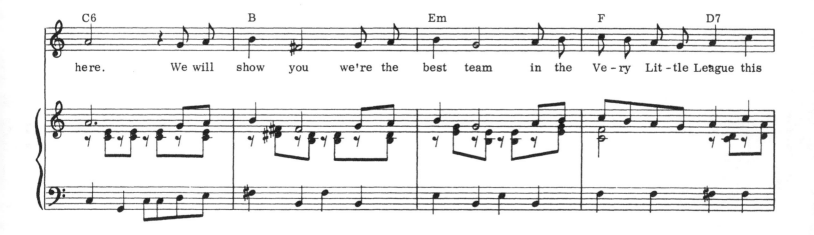

here. We will show you we're the best team in the Ve-ry Lit-tle League this

year. And in no time we'll be big time with the big league base-ball

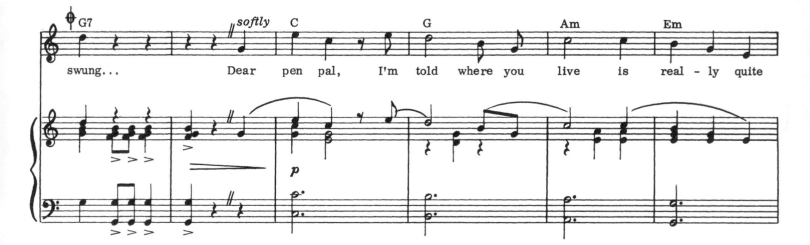

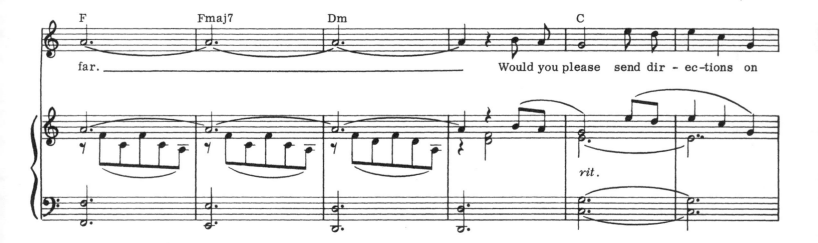

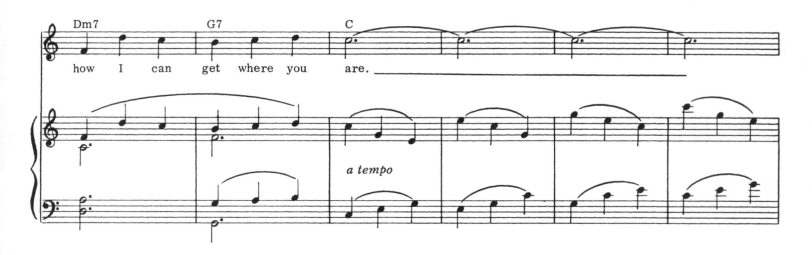

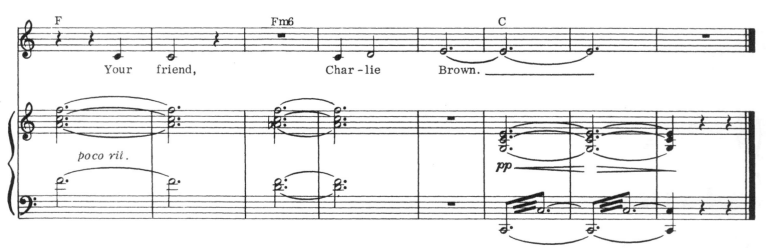

The Baseball Game - 5

THE KITE
(A/K/A CHARLIE BROWN'S KITE)

Words and Music by
CLARK GESNER

Quick, urgent

CB: Lit-tle more speed, lit-tle more rope,

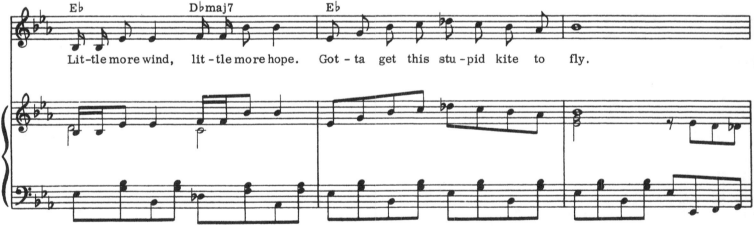

Lit-tle more wind, lit-tle more hope. Got-ta get this stu-pid kite to fly.

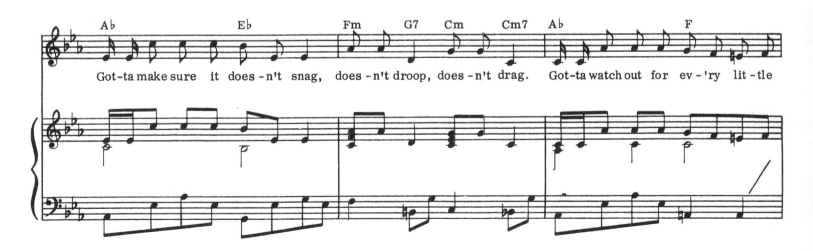

Got-ta make sure it does-n't snag, does-n't droop, does-n't drag. Got-ta watch out for ev-'ry lit-tle

The Kite - 5

The Kite - 5

The Kite - 5

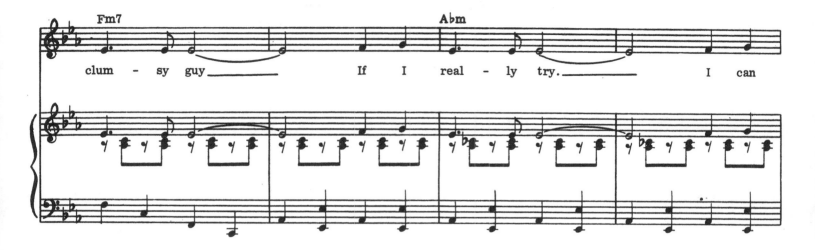

clum - sy guy _____ If I real - ly try. _____ I can

real - ly fly a...

(Tacet)

(Crunch)   *Lucy:* What happened to your kite, Charlie Brown,
it looks like it ran into a brick wall. (laugh)

pp   *a tempo*

ff   *tr*

LITTLE KNOWN FACTS

Words and Music by
CLARK GESNER

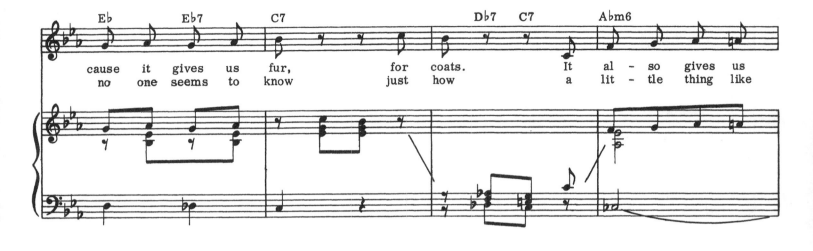

cause it gives us fur,   for coats.   It al - so gives us
no one seems to know   just how   a lit - tle thing like

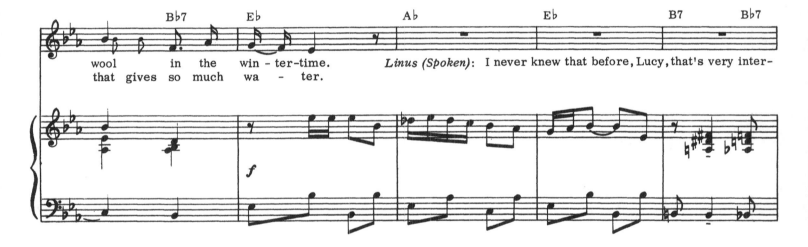

wool   in the win - ter-time.   *Linus (Spoken):* I never knew that before, Lucy, that's very inter-
that gives so much wa - ter.

esting.   *Lucy:* This is an elm tree.   It's ver - y lit - tle,
     D'you see that bird?   It's called an ea - gle;

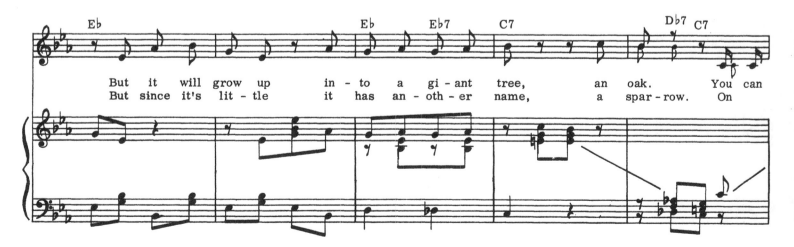

But it will grow up in - to a gi - ant tree, an oak. You can
But since it's lit - tle it has an - oth - er name, a spar - row. On

Little Known Facts - 4

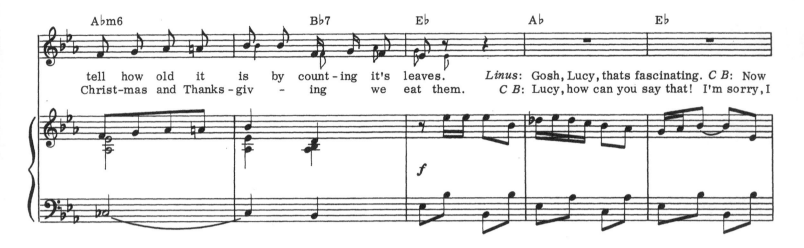

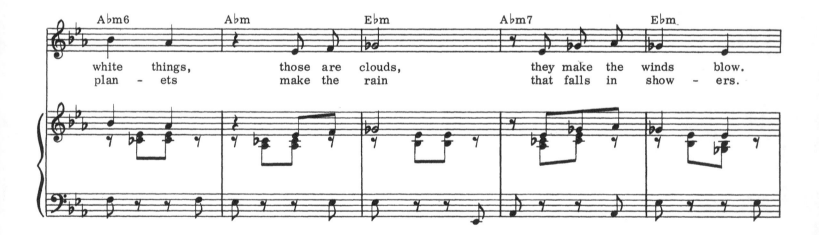

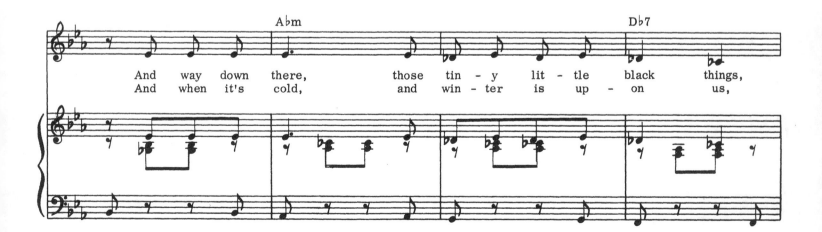

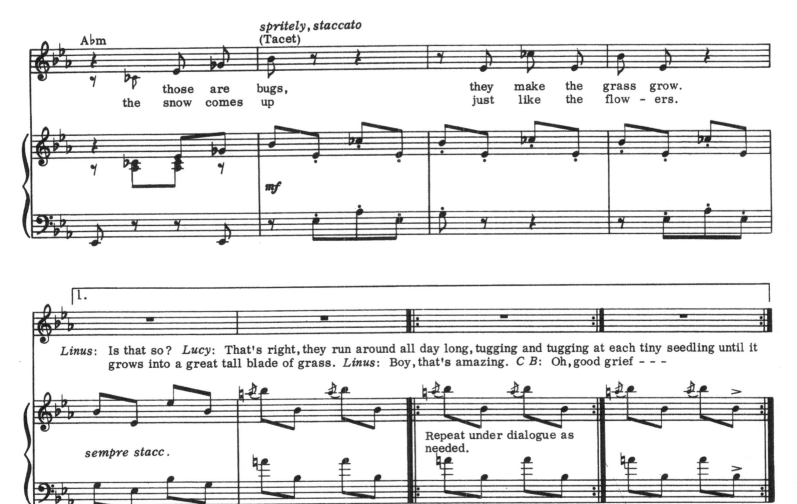

spritely, staccato
(Tacet)

the those are bugs,
the snow comes up

they make the grass grow.
just like the flow - ers.

1.

Linus: Is that so? *Lucy*: That's right, they run around all day long, tugging and tugging at each tiny seedling until it grows into a great tall blade of grass. *Linus*: Boy, that's amazing. *C B*: Oh, good grief - - -

sempre stacc.

Repeat under dialogue as needed.

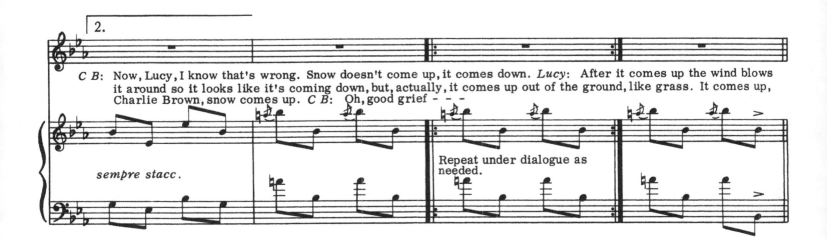

2.

C B: Now, Lucy, I know that's wrong. Snow doesn't come up, it comes down. *Lucy*: After it comes up the wind blows it around so it looks like it's coming down, but, actually, it comes up out of the ground, like grass. It comes up, Charlie Brown, snow comes up. *C B*: Oh, good grief - - -

sempre stacc.

Repeat under dialogue as needed.

Eb   Ab   Eb   B7   Bb7 Eb

Linus: Lucy, why is Charlie Brown banging his head against a tree?
Lucy: To loosen the bark so the tree will grow faster. Come along, Linus.

Little Known Facts - 4

SUPPERTIME

Words and Music by
CLARK GESNER

Suppertime - 5

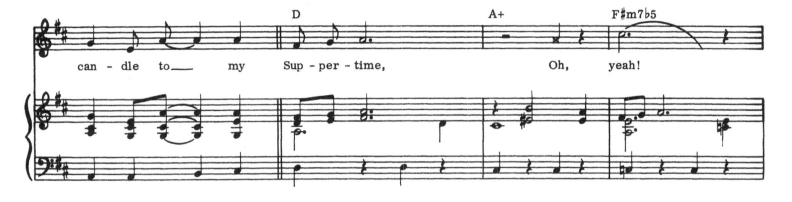

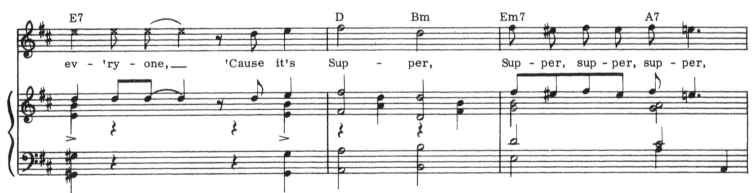

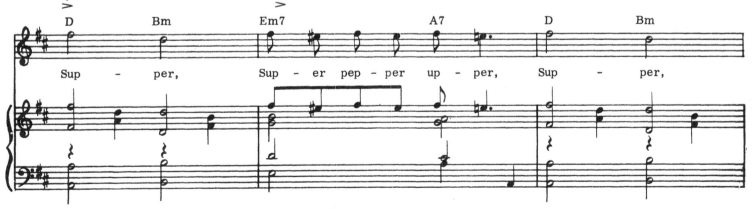

Snoopy - 5

Sup - er dup - er dup - per dup – a dup – a dup - a dup - a dup - a dup - a dup – a dup – a

Wild and noisy

(spoken) C B: Now, wait a minute, Snoopy. Hey, get down, you're

spilling it all over! Now cut that out! Why can't you eat your meal quietly and calmly like any other dog? Snoopy:(very softly) So, what's wrong with making mealtime a joy- ous occasion?

Snoopy: doo doo doo doo-de doo doo doo.__ (quietly)

HAPPINESS

Words and Music by
CLARK GESNER

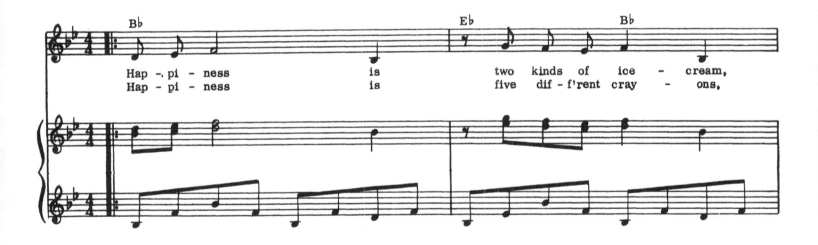

Hap -. pi - ness   is   two kinds of ice - cream,
Hap - pi - ness   is   five dif - f'rent cray - ons,

Find - ing your skate key,   tell - ing the time.
Know - ing a se - cret,   climb - ing a tree.

46

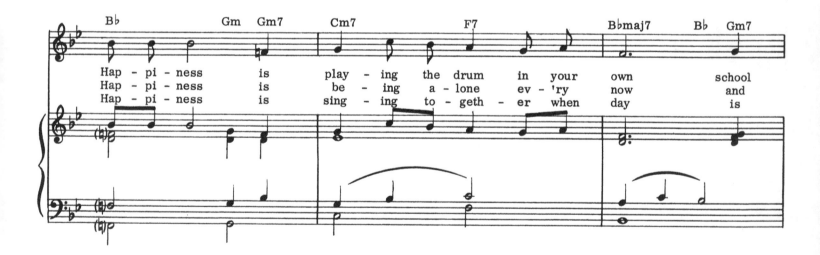

Happiness - 3

Happiness - 3